THE REMOTE LANDLORD

The Remote Landlord

THOMAS L MINOR

CONTENTS

| 1 |

The Evolution of Remote Property Management

Introduction

The property management industry has undergone a dramatic transformation over the past few decades, driven by technological advancements, changing tenant expectations, and evolving market dynamics. What was once a field reliant on in-person interactions, paper-based documentation, and localized management has now expanded into a dynamic, technology-driven industry where remote management is not only possible but often preferred.

This chapter explores the evolution of remote property management, from its early days of manual processes to the current landscape of automation, smart technology, and virtual oversight. Understanding this progression provides insight into the opportunities and challenges that modern property managers face in a digital world.

The Early Days: Traditional Property Management

In the past, property management was a hands-on, highly localized industry. Property owners or managers needed to be physically present to oversee maintenance, collect rent, and address tenant concerns. The key characteristics of early property management included:

- **On-Site Management:** Landlords or designated managers had to be physically available to inspect properties, conduct repairs, and interact with tenants.
- **Manual Record-Keeping:** Lease agreements, rent ledgers, and maintenance requests were all documented on paper, leading to inefficiencies and data loss.
- **Limited Communication Methods:** Landlords relied on phone calls, in-person visits, and mailed correspondence to interact with tenants.
- **Delayed Maintenance Response:** Without instant communication and digital tracking, addressing maintenance requests often took days or weeks.

These traditional practices made it difficult to manage multiple properties efficiently, particularly for owners with properties in different locations.

The Rise of Technology in Property Management (1990s – 2010s)

The late 20th century and early 21st century saw the emergence of technology that revolutionized the property management industry. Key innovations included:

1. The Internet and Email Communication

- Property managers could now communicate with tenants via email, reducing reliance on physical meetings.
- Digital lease agreements and online applications started replacing paper-based processes.

2. Property Management Software (PMS)

- Platforms like **Yardi, AppFolio, and Buildium** began offering digital rent collection, lease tracking, and maintenance scheduling.
- Cloud-based solutions allow managers to access information from anywhere, enabling the first steps toward remote property management.

3. Online Payment Systems

- The introduction of online rent payment methods, such as PayPal and automated bank transfers, streamlined rent collection.
- Property owners and managers no longer had to physically collect checks or cash.

4. Digital Marketing & Online Listings

- Websites like **Craigslist, Zillow, and Apartments.com** allow property managers to market rental units to a broader audience.
- Virtual tours and high-quality property photos replaced in-person showings, reducing the need for physical presence.

These advancements paved the way for a more remote-friendly approach to property management, but in-person interactions were still a significant part of the process.

The Remote Property Management Revolution (2010s – Present)

The past decade has marked the full-scale shift toward **remote property management**, with several key drivers leading the charge:

1. Smart Home Technology & IoT (Internet of Things)

- **Smart locks** allow landlords to grant and revoke access remotely, eliminating the need for physical keys.
- **Remote security cameras and smart sensors** provide real-time monitoring of properties.
- **Smart thermostats and energy management systems** help landlords reduce utility costs without being on-site.

2. AI-Powered Chatbots & Virtual Assistants

- Platforms like **AI leasing assistants and automated chatbots** handle tenant inquiries 24/7.
- AI-driven systems can screen potential tenants and recommend lease agreements based on financial and behavioral data.

3. Mobile Property Management Apps

- Apps such as **TenantCloud, RentRedi, and Cozy** allow landlords to manage their properties from anywhere.
- These apps integrate rent collection, maintenance requests, tenant screening, and financial reporting into a single platform.

4. Virtual Property Showings & Remote Leasing

- **3D virtual tours and augmented reality (AR)** enable prospective tenants to explore properties without visiting in person.
- Digital lease signing through **DocuSign and HelloSign** has eliminated the need for physical lease agreements.

5. Blockchain & Smart Contracts

- Blockchain technology is being explored for **tamper-proof lease agreements** and secure rent transactions.
- Smart contracts automatically enforce lease terms, such as triggering late fees when rent is overdue.

6. The Impact of COVID-19 on Remote Management

The pandemic significantly accelerated the adoption of remote property management tools. With social distancing measures in place, landlords and property managers were forced   to embrace:

- **Self-guided property tours with smart locks**
- **Online lease signings and digital notarization**
- **Remote maintenance coordination through third-party vendors**

This period demonstrated that **remote property management is not just a convenience but a necessity** in today's world.

The Future of Remote Property Management

As technology continues to advance, remote property management will become even more efficient and cost-effective. Some key trends to watch include:

- **AI-driven tenant screening and predictive analytics** to minimize risks and improve decision-making.
- **Metaverse and virtual property investments**, where landlords can manage digital assets in entirely new ways.
- **Fully automated rental experiences**, from AI-powered lease negotiations to self-repairing smart appliances.

With these innovations, property owners will have **unprecedented control over their real estate portfolios**, even if they never set foot on the properties they own.

Conclusion

The evolution of remote property management has transformed the industry from a hands-on, location-dependent business into a tech-driven, scalable operation. From the early days of manual processes to today's AI-driven, fully remote capabilities, the shift has empowered landlords, investors, and tenants alike.

Understanding this progression not only highlights the opportunities available in the modern property management landscape but also prepares industry professionals for the **next wave of digital transformation**. As new technologies emerge, remote property management will continue to evolve, creating **greater efficiency, profitability, and accessibility for real estate investors worldwide**.

| 2 |

Choosing the Right Property Management Software

A Guide to Selecting Tools for Seamless Operations

Managing rental properties effectively requires organization, efficiency, and a keen eye for detail. The right property management software (PMS) can streamline operations, automate tasks, and improve tenant satisfaction. In this chapter, we will explore the key considerations for selecting a PMS that aligns with your business needs, compare top software options, and discuss implementation best practices.

2.1 Understanding Your Needs

Before choosing property management software, it is crucial to identify your specific requirements. Consider the following:

2.1.1 Type of Property You Manage

- **Single-family homes**: May require lease tracking, online payments, and maintenance scheduling.
- **Multi-family units**: Needs tenant communication, automated billing, and work order management.

- **Commercial properties**: Requires lease administration, tenant billing, and financial reporting.
- **Short-term rentals**: Must integrate with booking platforms and offer dynamic pricing.

2.1.2 Business Size and Growth Goals

- If managing a few properties, a simple, cost-effective solution may suffice.
- For large portfolios or expansion plans, scalability and automation are key.

2.1.3 Key Features You Need

- **Tenant & Lease Management**: Automates lease tracking, renewals, and rent increases.
- **Online Payments**: Ensures tenants can pay rent electronically through multiple channels.
- **Maintenance Requests**: Allows tenants to submit issues and track progress in real-time.
- **Accounting & Financial Reporting**: Integrates with QuickBooks or other financial tools.
- **Tenant Screening**: Provides background checks, credit reports, and eviction history.
- **Communication Tools**: Includes automated reminders, emails, and in-app messaging.
- **Marketing & Listing Management**: Syncs vacancies with platforms like Zillow and Apartments.com.

2.2 Evaluating Software Options

With numerous software options available, selecting the right one requires research and comparison. Below are some of the most popular property management solutions:

2.2.1 Top Property Management Software

Software	Best For	Key Features	Pricing
Buildium	Small to mid-sized portfolios	Lease tracking, tenant screening, online payments, maintenance requests	Starts at $50/month
AppFolio	Large portfolios	AI-powered leasing, automated accounting, customizable reports	Starts at $280/month
TenantCloud	Budget-friendly, small landlords	Free basic plan, rent collection, tenant screening	Free, paid plans from $12/month
Rentec Direct	Mid-sized portfolios	QuickBooks integration, ACH payments, 1099 e-filing	Starts at $45/month
Yardi Breeze	Commercial & residential properties	CAM calculations, robust reporting, marketing tools	Starts at $100/month

Software	Best For	Key Features	Pricing
DoorLoop	All property types	Accounting, maintenance, tenant communication	Starts at $49/month

2.2.2 Factors to Consider When Comparing Options

- **Ease of Use**: Is the interface intuitive? Does it require extensive training?
- **Integration**: Does it work with your accounting software, CRM, or banking system?
- **Scalability**: Can it grow with your business?
- **Customer Support**: Is there 24/7 assistance or live chat?
- **Mobile Accessibility**: Can you manage operations from your phone?
- **Security & Compliance**: Does it have data encryption and compliance with housing regulations?

2.3 Implementing the Software Successfully

2.3.1 Setting Up the System

- Import property and tenant data.
- Configure lease terms, rent schedules, and security deposits.
- Integrate banking information for online payments.

2.3.2 Training Staff & Tenants

- Conduct staff training sessions or webinars.
- Provide tenants with user guides for rent payments and maintenance requests.

2.3.3 Monitoring and Optimizing Usage

- Regularly check reports to identify areas for improvement.
- Gather tenant and team feedback to enhance the user experience.
- Update software settings as business needs evolve.

Conclusion

Selecting the right property management software is a critical step in streamlining your rental business. By understanding your needs, evaluating options, and implementing the system effectively, you can optimize operations, enhance tenant satisfaction, and position your business for growth.

Action Steps

- List your must-have software features.
- Compare 2-3 software options with free trials.
- Develop an implementation plan for smooth adoption.

With the right software in place, managing rental properties becomes more efficient, allowing you to focus on growth and profitability.

| 3 |

Virtual Assistants in Property Management

How AI and Remote Assistants Streamline Tasks

Introduction

The remote landlord landscape looks very different from just a few years ago. Artificial intelligence (AI) and virtual assistants (VAs) have moved from curiosities to everyday tools that are reshaping how rental portfolios are managed. Analysts estimate that the global market for AI in real estate will climb from roughly $222 billion in 2024 to more than $303 billion in 2025. In parallel, the services market for human virtual assistants is exploding – it is expected to jump from about $5 billion in 2023 to more than $15 billion by 2028. Property managers are embracing these tools because they cut costs, free up time and help scale operations. Nearly nine in ten third-party property-management companies plan to expand their portfolios in 2024–25, and the share of single-family homes built specifically for rent has almost doubled since 2021. To thrive in this competitive environment, you must leverage technology.

At the same time, the regulatory and social landscape has shifted. New laws like California's AB 2801 require landlords with 16 or more units to offer rent-payment reporting to credit bureaus and to document unit conditions with timestamped photos; other jurisdictions are banning hidden fees and "no-grounds" evictions. Fair-housing enforcement is tightening, with initiatives ranging from "ban-the-box" policies that restrict the use of criminal histories in tenant screening to oversight of algorithmic bias in resident-screening tools. Tenant expectations are rising – they want 24/7 access to services, energy-efficient homes, transparent fees and inclusive communities. Against this backdrop, AI and remote assistants aren't just conveniences; they're the keys to delivering responsive service while staying compliant and profitable.

This chapter takes a forward-looking look at how AI-powered tools and human virtual assistants are streamlining every aspect of property management. We'll cover the rise of virtual assistants, the latest AI innovations, the irreplaceable human roles, and how to choose the right mix of tools for your portfolio. Throughout, we'll be blunt about the challenges – from data-privacy concerns to ethical screening – and offer practical steps to stay ahead.

3.1 The Rise of Virtual Assistants in Real Estate

Virtual assistance isn't new, but its adoption in real estate has exploded. Demand is being driven by remote work, a shortage of onsite talent and a need to operate around the clock. Surveys show that roughly two-thirds of users hire virtual assistants to save time, more than half use them to delegate tasks, and nearly half cite increased productivity. Companies also hire VAs to reduce stress, improve work-life balance and access specialized skills. The appeal isn't just qualitative; VAs can slash operating costs by as much as 70–78% by eliminating office overhead and payroll expenses. In fact, virtual assistants are so effective that 63% of users now prefer them over in-office assistants, and satisfaction is high – 91% of clients rate their VAs as excellent or good.

Real estate is one of the fastest-growing sectors for remote assistance, accounting for about 5% of the global VA market. Adoption of AI-powered chat and support tools is also surging; 28% of real-estate firms have already embraced live chat technology and more than 72% of owners are either planning or actively investing in AI. Consumers expect this level of service – nine out of ten customers now anticipate businesses will use conversational assistants, and 43% of customer-experience experts report rising demand for immediate responses. Simply put, VAs and chatbots are no longer optional; they're table stakes if you want to compete in 2025.

Key benefits of virtual assistants for property managers include:

- **Cost savings:** Hiring full-time onsite staff is expensive. Virtual assistants and AI bots work on demand, letting you pay per task or hour. They also eliminate expenses like office space, equipment and employee benefits.
- **Time efficiency:** Delegating repetitive tasks – from tenant inquiries to invoice reconciliation – frees up your schedule for strategic planning and acquisitions.
- **Scalability:** As your portfolio grows, you can add more assistants or upgrade to more powerful AI tools without the headaches of traditional hiring.
- **24/7 availability:** Bots never sleep. They answer questions, schedule tours and troubleshoot issues at any hour, giving your rental business global reach and keeping tenants satisfied.
- **Regulatory compliance and documentation:** Today's AI-powered systems automatically maintain audit trails, store

timestamped photos, record communications and even report rent payments to credit bureaus, helping you comply with new laws.

3.2 How AI is Changing Property Management

AI isn't just automating tasks – it's transforming how properties are marketed, managed and monetized. Below are the major areas where AI is making an impact.

3.2.1 AI-Powered Chatbots and Conversational Assistants

Modern property chatbots are more than FAQs. Using natural language processing and generative AI, these bots engage prospects, qualify leads, schedule tours and even perform initial tenant screenings. They operate across websites, SMS and social-media platforms and can integrate with calendar and CRM systems. More importantly, they deliver immediate responses – a critical advantage when 90% of consumers expect businesses to deploy conversational assistants. Live chat adoption in real estate already stands at 28%, and the bots keep improving. They can personalize recommendations based on user preferences, send follow-up messages automatically and provide interactive virtual tours of floor plans – a feature that resonates with 55% of homebuyers. On the cost side, chatbots can reduce customer-service expenses by up to 30% and save companies billions in salary costs. In short, they're a must-have for any modern rental operation.

3.2.2 Lease and Document Automation & Smart Contracts

AI-driven document-automation tools now do more than mail-merge leases. They can abstract key clauses, flag risky terms and automatically populate rent schedules. Platforms like DocuSign and HelloSign remain staples, but new AI tools can summarize 40-page leases into bullet points and identify regulatory gaps. Some property-management suites are experimenting with smart contracts that leverage blockchain to execute lease clauses automatically – for example, releasing security deposits when move-out inspection photos are approved. RealCube forecasts that AI combined with blockchain will allow self-executing rent payments and lease agreements. These innovations dovetail with regulatory changes requiring landlords to document unit conditions with timestamped photos and to report rent payments to credit bureaus. Automated documentation not only reduces clerical work but also protects you in disputes and helps meet fair-housing standards.

3.2.3 Predictive Maintenance and IoT Integration

AI algorithms trained on historical work orders can now predict when a boiler will fail or an HVAC system needs servicing. But predictive maintenance really shines when combined with the Internet of Things (IoT). Smart building sensors monitor temperature, humidity and vibration; AI analyses that data in real time to detect anomalies. RealCube notes that AI-powered sensors can identify equipment problems before they become serious and automatically assign tickets to technicians based on severity and availability. The result is fewer emergency repairs, longer asset life and happier tenants. IoT also enables energy optimization; sensors adjust lighting and HVAC based on occupancy and weather, cutting utility costs and boosting sustainability. As more appliances become connected, expect predictive maintenance to become standard practice.

3.2.4 Automated Rent Collection and Financial Management

AI-integrated payment systems handle rent collection, send reminders, apply late fees and reconcile bank deposits automatically. They also flag delinquent accounts and can even initiate notices consistent with local law. Regulation is prompting further innovation: states like California now ban certain junk fees and require transparency when charging tenants for payment methods. Automated systems make it easier to comply by itemizing charges and keeping digital records. Voice-enabled dashboards are on the horizon; Real-Cube predicts that property managers will soon be able to check collections or approve invoices using voice commands. VAs trained in bookkeeping can complement these tools by categorizing expenses in software like QuickBooks or Buildium and generating real-time financial reports.

3.2.5 Market Analysis, Pricing Optimization & Big Data

Setting the right rent is both art and science. Modern AI platforms digest millions of data points – comparable rents, vacancy rates, seasonal demand, economic indicators and even crime statistics – to recommend optimal pricing. Services like Zillow's Rent Zestimate use machine-learning models to provide instant valuations. Predictive AI analytics can forecast future rental prices and identify emerging neighborhoods. This is particularly important as built-for-rent single-family homes gain market share; landlords need to know when to raise rents or offer incentives. Advanced search tools like RealScout allow tenants to find homes based on proximity to schools, workplaces or amenities, providing landlords with real-time insights into tenant preferences. In the near future, expect AI systems to combine market analysis with personalized marketing campaigns to target high-value prospects automatically.

3.2.6 Smart Homes, Sustainability and ESG

Energy-efficient housing isn't just a feel-good feature – it's a competitive advantage. A survey by the Urban Land Institute found that 73% of renters are willing to pay more for energy-efficient housing. IoT-enabled thermostats, keyless entry systems and smart lighting not only reduce utility bills but also deliver the convenience modern tenants expect. AI monitors energy consumption across your portfolio, identifies waste and suggests upgrades. RealCube foresees AI dashboards that track sustainability metrics like carbon emissions and waste management. Human VAs can spearhead green initiatives by researching LED retrofits, coordinating recycling programs and managing renewable energy projects. Investing in smart, sustainable features satisfies tenant demand, lowers operating costs and positions your properties to meet emerging ESG (Environmental, Social and Governance) standards.

3.2.7 Fair-Housing Compliance and Ethical AI

Technology must be used responsibly. New laws are forcing property managers to increase transparency and eliminate discrimination. Fair-housing policies in 2025 include "ban-the-box" rules that limit consideration of criminal histories, language-access requirements, oversight of algorithmic bias in screening, disclosure of environmental risks and expanded accommodations for disabilities. Landlords in many jurisdictions are also required to document unit conditions and provide rent-reporting to credit bureaus. Some regions allow tenants to change locks if safety concerns aren't addressed promptly and bans on hidden fees and no-grounds evictions are becoming more common. To meet these obligations, property managers should adopt AI-powered screening tools that evaluate applicants objectively and regularly audit those tools for bias. Digital checklists and photo documentation systems ensure that move-in and move-out inspections are thorough and transparent. VAs can help by keeping up with legislation, ensuring documentation is complete and scheduling training for onsite teams. Remember: compliance isn't optional – fines, lawsuits and reputational damage are rising.

3.3 The Role of Human Virtual Assistants in Property Management

AI is powerful, but there are things only humans can do. Remote assistants bring empathy, judgement and creativity to situations that require nuance. Their role has expanded beyond basic admin support to include strategic tasks across the entire property lifecycle:

1. **Tenant screening and leasing:** VAs can verify employment, income and references, run credit checks, and ensure screening complies with fair-housing laws. They also prepare lease documents, collect digital signatures and arrange move-in appointments. Because of "ban-the-box" rules and increased oversight of screening algorithms, having a human review edge cases reduces legal risk.

2. **Marketing and lead generation:** VAs craft compelling listings, manage social-media campaigns, respond to inquiries and coordinate virtual tours. They can integrate chatbots and AI tools to qualify leads faster while still providing the human touch that builds trust. With short-term rentals and co-living spaces growing rapidly – demand for short-term rentals surged 24% last year – VAs are invaluable in keeping calendars full and guests happy.

3. **Maintenance coordination and 24/7 tenant support:** Remote assistants log maintenance requests, triage issues and dispatch vendors. They confirm completion, follow up with tenants and update maintenance records. This round-the-clock coordination addresses rising tenant expectations for quick resolutions and ensures you stay compliant with new laws granting tenants lock-change rights and other protections.

4. **Bookkeeping, reporting and rent collection:** VAs reconcile invoices, categorize expenses, prepare monthly statements and ensure rent payments are recorded correctly. They also monitor compliance with rent-reporting requirements and document fees in jurisdictions that ban certain charges. Integrating a skilled VA with AI-powered accounting tools gives you real-time financial insight and audit trails.

5. **Sustainability and ESG initiatives:** Beyond keeping the books, VAs can spearhead green programs. They research energy-efficient

upgrades, coordinate waste-reduction efforts, manage water-conservation systems and track renewable-energy options. They also communicate these initiatives to tenants, increasing engagement and willingness to pay a premium for eco-friendly housing.

6. **Regulatory compliance and legal support:** Virtual assistants keep track of fair-housing laws, rent-control updates and eviction rules. They schedule inspections, draft notices and assemble documentation for attorneys. In an era of increasing regulation, having a knowledgeable assistant ensures you don't miss critical deadlines or overlook new requirements.

7. **Community building and tenant relations:** Modern property management isn't just about collecting rent. VAs manage newsletters, organize resident events, mediate disputes and collect feedback. They play a crucial role in creating inclusive communities that reflect fair-housing principles and tenant expectations.

3.4 Choosing the Right Virtual Assistants and AI Tools

With so many options, how do you build your remote-management stack? Here's a framework to guide your decisions:

1. **Define your goals and compliance needs.** Identify the tasks you want to automate or delegate – rent collection, maintenance dispatch, marketing, sustainability, compliance – and consider your regulatory environment. Do you operate in a jurisdiction with rent-reporting requirements or strict fair-housing rules? Your choice of tools should align with these obligations.

2. **Evaluate AI platforms and software.** Beyond well-known platforms like Buildium, AppFolio and Cozy, new contenders are emerging. RealCube's NOVA engine delivers AI-driven dashboards, automated maintenance scheduling and predictive analytics. Real-

Scout offers AI-powered property searches and personalized recommendations. Showdigs automates in-person and virtual tour scheduling, while Yardi and RealPage incorporate AI for pricing and marketing. Look for solutions that integrate with your existing CRM, accounting and IoT systems.

3. **Hire skilled virtual assistants.** Experience matters. Seek candidates with property-management, customer-service or real-estate marketing backgrounds. Platforms like Upwork, Fiverr and OnlineJobs.ph remain popular, but also consider agencies specializing in real-estate VAs. Pay attention to location: while offshore talent can be cost-effective, surveys show that 76% of users prefer onshore assistants for sensitive tasks. Ensure that any VA you hire is trained in fair-housing laws, privacy protocols and sustainability best practices.

4. **Blend AI with human expertise.** The most effective operations use AI to handle repetitive tasks and a human team to manage exceptions, build relationships and oversee compliance. For example, a chatbot can answer basic questions and schedule viewings, but a human VA should handle lease negotiations or sensitive tenant disputes. Likewise, an AI rent-payment system can process transactions, but a VA should review unusual payment issues or assist tenants who need help.

5. **Monitor performance and adapt.** Set clear metrics for your AI tools (response time, conversion rate, maintenance resolution time) and your VAs (task completion, tenant satisfaction). Conduct regular audits to ensure your screening algorithms aren't introducing bias. Update training as regulations change. The landscape is evolving quickly – be ready to adjust your toolkit as new technologies like voice-enabled dashboards and smart-contracts mature.

Conclusion

AI-powered tools and human virtual assistants are no longer futuristic add-ons; they're core components of a competitive property-management strategy. The market for these technologies is booming, and tenants increasingly expect tech-driven convenience, green living and transparent processes. At the same time, governments are imposing stricter rules around rent reporting, fee disclosures and fair-housing compliance. By embracing automation for routine tasks, leveraging predictive analytics for maintenance and pricing, investing in smart-home and sustainability upgrades, and pairing all of that with empathetic human assistants, you'll deliver better service and protect your bottom line. Don't expect the pace of change to slow – voice-enabled dashboards, AI-driven sustainability insights and blockchain-based leases are on the horizon. Adapting early isn't optional; it's the difference between thriving and falling behind in the remote-landlord era.

| 4 |

Automating Rent Collection and Expense Tracking

Tools and Techniques for Financial Management

Introduction

Effective financial management is essential for any real estate investor, and automation is the key to efficiency and scalability. Automating rent collection and expense tracking not only saves time but also ensures accuracy, reduces errors, and improves cash flow management. This chapter explores various tools, platforms, and strategies to streamline rent collection and expense tracking for your rental properties.

4.1 The Importance of Automating Financial Management

Manual rent collection and expense tracking can be time-consuming, prone to human error, and difficult to scale as your portfolio grows. Automation offers several benefits, including:

- **Efficiency:** Saves time by reducing manual entry and processing.
- **Accuracy:** Minimizes errors in calculations and record-keeping.
- **Convenience:** Enables tenants to pay rent easily and landlords to track finances in real time.
- **Cash Flow Stability:** Reduces late payments and ensures timely receipt of rent.
- **Compliance and Documentation:** Helps maintain accurate financial records for tax reporting and business growth.

By leveraging technology, landlords can streamline operations and focus on scaling their real estate investment business.

4.2 Automating Rent Collection

4.2.1 Online Payment Platforms

The traditional method of collecting rent via checks or cash is inefficient. Digital payment solutions offer faster and more reliable alternatives. Some of the best rent collection platforms include:
  1. **Avail**

- Free for landlords, with an option for tenants to pay rent via bank transfer (ACH) or credit/debit card.
- Automates reminders and late fee enforcement.
- Integrates with accounting software for financial tracking.

2. Cozy (Now Part of Apartments.com)

- Allows tenants to set up automatic payments.
- Provides financial reporting tools for landlords.
- Offers a free option with paid add-ons.

3. Buildium

- A comprehensive property management software with auto-mated rent collection.
- Allows direct deposit into your account.
- Generates financial reports for tax purposes.

4. TurboTenant

- Free for landlords, with a small processing fee for tenants.
- Sends automatic reminders and payment confirmations.
- Includes screening tools for prospective tenants.

5. RentRedi

- Works with various payment methods, including ACH, credit cards, and even cash (via PayNearMe).
- Syncs with QuickBooks for accounting integration.
- Includes features like autopay and eviction alerts.

4.2.2 Setting Up Automated Payments

To maximize efficiency, follow these steps to automate rent collection:

1. **Choose a rental collection platform** that fits your needs.
2. **Set up recurring payments** so tenants can opt for automatic withdrawals.

3. **Implement late fee policies** that are automatically applied when payments are overdue.
4. **Send automated reminders** via email or SMS a few days before rent is due.
5. **Monitor payments in real time** using your chosen platform's dashboard.

Encouraging tenants to enroll in automatic payments significantly reduces late payments and improves cash flow stability.

4.3 Automating Expense Tracking

4.3.1 Expense Tracking Software

Tracking expenses manually can be overwhelming, especially when managing multiple properties. The following tools help automate and categorize expenses efficiently:

1. Stessa

- Designed specifically for real estate investors.
- Tracks income and expenses automatically by syncing with bank accounts.
- Generates reports for tax filing and financial analysis.

2. QuickBooks Online

- One of the most powerful accounting tools, with real estate-specific features.
- Integrates with rent collection platforms like Buildium and RentRedi.
- Provides customizable reports for expense tracking and tax preparation.

3. AppFolio

- A complete property management solution with built-in expense tracking.
- Automates financial reporting and integrates with accounting software.
- Ideal for landlords with multiple properties.

4. Wave Accounting

- Free accounting software with invoicing and receipt scanning features.
- Suitable for landlords managing a small portfolio.
- Syncs with bank accounts automatically categorize transactions.

4.3.2 Automating Bill Payments

Landlords often deal with multiple recurring expenses, such as:

- **Mortgage payments**
- **Property taxes**
- **Insurance premiums**
- **Utility bills (if not paid by tenants)**
- **Property maintenance and repairs**

To automate bill payments:

1. **Use bank autopay services** for fixed monthly expenses like mortgage payments.
2. **Set up automatic bill payments** through property management software or accounting tools.
3. **Link utility bills and service providers** to online payment platforms for seamless transactions.
4. **Schedule recurring transfers** to a dedicated maintenance fund to cover emergency repairs.

Automating these expenses ensures that all financial obligations are met on time, preventing late fees or service disruptions.

4.4 Integrating Rent Collection with Expense Tracking

For a seamless financial workflow, landlords should integrate rent collection with expense tracking. Here's how:

1. **Use software that supports both functions** – Platforms like Buildium, AppFolio, and Stessa allow rent collection and expense tracking in one place.
2. **Sync payment platforms with accounting tools** – Many rent collection platforms integrate with QuickBooks or Wave for automatic financial updates.
3. **Categorize transactions automatically** – Set up rules in accounting software to assign expenses to relevant categories (e.g., repairs, utilities, property taxes).
4. **Generate automated reports** – Use financial dashboards to monitor income, expenses, and cash flow trends.

A well-integrated system provides real-time insights into profitability and helps make informed investment decisions.

4.5 Leveraging AI and Smart Automation

Artificial intelligence (AI) is transforming financial management in real estate. Some cutting-edge automation tools include:

- **Enzo AI Property Manager** – Uses AI to predict late payments and optimize rent collection.
- **Pluto Money Manager** – An AI-driven tool that categorizes expenses and provides cash flow forecasts.

- **AI-powered chatbots** – Handle tenant inquiries about payments and send reminders.

Landlords who embrace AI and automation can manage their properties more efficiently and increase profitability.

4.6 Common Challenges and How to Overcome Them

Despite the advantages, landlords may face challenges when automating financial management:

1. **Tenant Resistance to Digital Payments**
   - Solution: Offer incentives for tenants who set up auto-pay, such as a small discount or fee waiver.
2. **Technical Issues with Payment Platforms**
   - Solution: Choose a platform with strong customer support and backup payment options.
3. **Difficulty Categorizing Expenses**
   - Solution: Use software with AI-powered categorization and set up predefined expense categories.
4. **Cash Flow Gaps Due to Late Payments**
   - Solution: Implement late fees and use rent guarantee services for added security.

By addressing these challenges, landlords can ensure a smooth transition to automated financial management.

Final Thoughts

Automation is no longer a luxury—it's a necessity for real estate investors looking to scale efficiently. By leveraging digital rent collection tools, automated expense tracking software, and AI-driven insights, landlords can improve financial management, reduce stress, and focus on growing their portfolios.

Action Steps:

- Choose and implement a rent collection platform.
- Integrate expense tracking software into your business.
- Automate bill payments to reduce manual work.
- Regularly review financial reports for insights and optimizations.

By following these strategies, you'll create a financially sound and scalable real estate business that maximizes cash flow and minimizes administrative burden.

| 5 |

Implementing Keyless Entry and Smart Security

Enhancing Tenant Experience and Security Remotely

Introduction

In today's rental market, technology plays a crucial role in improving tenant satisfaction and property security. Implementing keyless entry systems and smart security solutions not only enhances convenience but also provides landlords and property managers with greater control over their properties. This chapter explores the benefits, implementation strategies, and best practices for integrating smart security solutions into rental properties.

5.1 The Benefits of Keyless Entry and Smart Security

Convenience for Tenants

Traditional keys can be easily lost, copied, or misplaced, leading to security concerns and unnecessary costs for landlords. Keyless entry solutions allow tenants to access their units using smartphone apps, PIN codes, or biometric authentication, eliminating the need for physical keys.

Enhanced Security

Smart locks and security systems provide real-time access control and monitoring. With features such as time-restricted access and activity logs, landlords can track who enters and exits the property. Additionally, temporary codes can be generated for maintenance personnel, service providers, or short-term rental guests.

Remote Management for Landlords

For landlords managing multiple properties or operating remotely, keyless entry systems reduce the need for in-person interactions to handle lost keys, lockouts, or move-ins/move-outs. Smart security systems allow for remote monitoring via mobile apps, increasing efficiency and reducing operational costs.

Cost Savings and Reduced Liability

Rekeying locks between tenants can be expensive and time-consuming. With keyless entry, landlords can change access codes digitally, eliminating the need for locksmith services. Additionally, a well-secured property reduces the risk of break-ins, which can lead to insurance savings.

5.2 Selecting the Right Keyless Entry System

When choosing a keyless entry system, consider the following factors:

Types of Keyless Entry Systems

1. **Smart Locks with Keypad Access** – Tenants can enter a PIN code to unlock the door. Some models allow landlords to generate one-time or recurring codes for different users.
2. **Bluetooth or Wi-Fi-Enabled Smart Locks** – These locks connect to a tenant's smartphone via Bluetooth or Wi-Fi, allowing remote access.
3. **Biometric Locks** – These use fingerprint recognition, ensuring that only authorized individuals can access the unit.
4. **RFID Card Readers** – Common in multi-unit buildings, these systems use RFID cards or fobs for access.
5. **Intercom and Video Doorbells** – Integrated systems allow tenants to verify visitors remotely and grant access via a mobile app.

Integration with Property Management Systems

To maximize efficiency, choose a keyless entry system that integrates with your property management software. Some platforms offer automatic access code generation upon lease signing and automatic deactivation after a lease expires.

Backup Access Options

Ensure that smart locks have a backup entry method, such as a physical key override or emergency battery access, to prevent lockouts in case of system failure.

5.3 Implementing Smart Security Systems

Smart Cameras and Surveillance

Installing smart cameras at entry points, parking areas, and shared spaces provides added security. Look for features such as:

- Motion detection alerts
- Cloud storage for recorded footage
- Remote viewing through a mobile app
- Two-way audio for communication

Motion Sensors and Smart Alarms

Smart motion sensors and alarms can detect unauthorized entry and trigger alerts. Some systems integrate with law enforcement or security services for emergency response.

Environmental Sensors for Property Protection

To protect the property from damage, consider adding:

- **Water leak sensors** – Detect plumbing leaks before they cause significant damage.
- **Smart smoke and carbon monoxide detectors** – Send mobile alerts to landlords and tenants in case of fire or gas leaks.
- **Temperature and humidity sensors** – Prevent issues like frozen pipes or mold growth.

5.4 Best Practices for Implementation

Educating Tenants on Smart Security Usage

Provide tenants with clear instructions on how to use keyless entry systems and smart security features. A simple onboarding process can include:

- A printed or digital guide on accessing their unit
- A tutorial video on mobile app features
- A support contact for troubleshooting issues

Addressing Privacy Concerns

Tenants may have concerns about surveillance and data privacy. Ensure that cameras are placed only in public areas (never inside units) and clarify data usage policies in the lease agreement.

Regular System Maintenance and Updates

Like any technology, smart locks and security systems require regular updates and maintenance. Set a schedule for:

- Checking battery levels in smart locks
- Updating firmware for security patches
- Verifying that surveillance systems are operational

Compliance with Local Regulations

Some states and municipalities have regulations regarding electronic locks, tenant privacy, and security system usage. Always ensure compliance with local housing laws and tenant rights.

5.5 Case Studies: Successful Implementation of Keyless Entry and Smart Security

Case Study 1: Single-Family Rental Property

A landlord managing a single-family rental home implemented a Wi-Fi-enabled smart lock. Tenants appreciated the ease of access and remote-control features, while the landlord reduced key replacement costs and improved security.

Case Study 2: Multi-Unit Apartment Complex

A property management company replaced traditional locks with RFID card access and installed smart surveillance cameras in common areas. The result was a 40% decrease in unauthorized access and improved tenant satisfaction.

Case Study 3: Short-Term Rental Property

A landlord managing a vacation rental installed a smart lock with a rotating access code system. Each guest received a unique, time-limited code, streamlining the check-in process and enhancing security.

5.6 Future Trends in Keyless Entry and Smart Security

The real estate industry is continuously evolving with advancements in smart security technology. Emerging trends include:

- **AI-Powered Security Systems** – Using machine learning to detect unusual activity patterns.
- **Blockchain-Based Access Control** – Providing tamper-proof, decentralized security authentication.
- **Smart Home Automation Integration** – Connecting security with other smart devices like lighting and HVAC systems for improved energy efficiency and safety.

Conclusion

Implementing keyless entry and smart security systems is a forward-thinking approach to property management that enhances tenant experience while improving security. By choosing the right technologies, educating tenants, and maintaining compliance with local laws, landlords can streamline operations and add value to their rental properties. As smart security solutions continue to evolve, staying updated on the latest innovations will ensure long-term success in the rental market.

| 6 |

Remote Tenant Screening and Lease Signing

Ensuring You Get the Right Tenants
Without Being On-Site

Introduction

As a real estate investor, particularly in rental properties, ensuring you have the right tenants is crucial to maintaining profitability and minimizing risks. Remote tenant screening and lease signing have become essential in today's digital landscape, allowing landlords to efficiently fill vacancies without the need to be physically present. This chapter covers the key steps, tools, and best practices to help you secure responsible tenants while managing the process remotely.

1. The Importance of Tenant Screening

Tenant screening is your first line of defense against late payments, property damage, and eviction costs. A strong screening process ensures you select tenants who:

- Pay rent on time
- Follow lease terms
- Maintain the property
- Have a history of responsible tenancy

With remote rental management, screening becomes even more critical as you won't be able to meet the tenant in person before they move in.

2. Essential Criteria for Tenant Selection

To ensure consistency and compliance with Fair Housing Laws, establish clear selection criteria, such as:

- **Credit Score & Financial Stability**: A credit score of 650+ is ideal, but flexible standards may be applied based on rental history and income.
- **Income Verification**: Rent should not exceed 30-40% of the tenant's gross income.
- **Rental History**: No evictions, frequent late payments, or property damage history.
- **Criminal Background Check**: While non-discriminatory, ensure there are no serious offenses that could pose a risk.
- **Employment Verification**: Confirm steady income through employer verification or tax returns for self-employed applicants.

3. Digital Tools for Remote Tenant Screening

Several online platforms allow landlords to conduct thorough background checks remotely:

- **TransUnion SmartMove** – Provides credit, criminal, and eviction reports.
- **MyRental by CoreLogic** – Offers detailed risk assessment scores.
- **RentPrep** – Conducts customizable background checks.
- **Zillow Rental Manager** – Includes tenant screening with application processing.

These tools allow you to collect applicant information, run background checks, and assess risk factors without needing in-person interactions.

4. Virtual Showings and Property Tours

Since you're screening tenants remotely, providing a clear picture of the property is key. Consider:

- **Pre-recorded Video Tours**: Walk through the property while narrating key features.
- **Live Virtual Showings**: Use Zoom, FaceTime, or Google Meet to give real-time tours and answer questions.
- **360° Virtual Walkthroughs**: Services like Matterport or Zillow 3D Home create interactive tours.

This approach saves time, ensures transparency, and helps tenants make informed decisions.

5. Online Rental Applications

Encourage prospective tenants to complete an online rental application to streamline the process. Use platforms such as:

- Zillow Rental Manager
- Apartments.com
- Avail.co
- TurboTenant

These applications typically collect:

- Personal information
- Employment details
- Rental history
- References

Automating this step makes the process efficient and ensures consistency.

6. Conducting Remote Interviews

Even with strong screening tools, a brief virtual interview can help assess a tenant's demeanor and verify information. Some key questions to ask:

- Why are you moving?
- When would you like to move in?
- Do you have any pets?
- What is your typical monthly income?
- Have you ever been evicted? If so, what were the circumstances?
- Can you provide references from your previous landlord?

A short 10-15 minute video call using Zoom or FaceTime can give you valuable insights.

7. Lease Agreement and Digital Signing

Once you've selected a tenant, lease signing can be completed remotely. Steps include:

1. **Draft a Legally Sound Lease Agreement** – Use state-specific templates from platforms like Rocket Lawyer or LawDepot.
2. **Send Lease for Digital Signing** – Use **DocuSign, HelloSign, or Adobe Sign** to allow tenants to sign electronically.
3. **Verify Identity** – Request a government-issued ID to confirm identity before finalizing.
4. **Collect Security Deposit and First Month's Rent** – Use **Zelle, PayPal, Venmo, or property management software** to receive payments securely.
5. **Provide Digital Copies** – Send a final copy of the lease agreement via email.

8. Setting Up Remote Rent Payments

To make ongoing rent collection seamless, establish digital payment methods. Consider:

- **Property Management Software**: Buildium, AppFolio, or RentRedi.
- **Direct Transfers**: Zelle, PayPal, or ACH transfers.
- **Automated Payment Systems**: Set up recurring payments to ensure on-time rent collection.

Encourage tenants to use automatic payments to avoid late fees.

9. Implementing Remote Move-In Procedures

Once the lease is signed, coordinate a smooth move-in process:

- **Smart Locks or Lockboxes**: Provide digital access codes or use lockboxes like Master Lock for key pickup.
- **Pre-Move-In Checklist**: Share a digital checklist detailing move-in expectations.
- **Welcome Packet**: Email key details such as trash schedules, maintenance contacts, and house rules.

This method reduces physical interaction while ensuring tenants feel supported.

10. Legal Considerations & Compliance

To avoid legal issues:

- Ensure compliance with **Fair Housing Laws** to prevent discrimination.
- Follow **state-specific security deposit laws** regarding holding and returning deposits.
- Use legally binding **electronic lease agreements** that comply with the **E-SIGN Act**.

Consult with a real estate attorney or use property management software to ensure legal compliance.

11. Handling Remote Tenant Issues

Once tenants move in, you may need to address maintenance, complaints, or lease violations remotely. Best practices include:

- **Property Management Software** – Tracks issues and automates maintenance requests.
- **Local Contractors & Handymen** – Have a reliable network to handle repairs.
- **Regular Virtual Check-Ins** – Use video calls or tenant surveys to address concerns.

By maintaining strong communication, you can effectively manage tenant relationships from anywhere.

Conclusion

Remote tenant screening and lease signing are crucial for modern real estate investors who want to manage properties efficiently without being on-site. By leveraging technology, automation, and best practices, you can ensure you attract responsible tenants while maintaining compliance and minimizing risks.

With the right tools and processes in place, managing rental properties remotely can be a seamless and profitable experience.

| 7 |

Using Local Realtors and Property Managers

Using Local Realtors and Property Managers Effectively

Introduction

Building a strong local team is one of the most crucial steps in achieving success in real estate investing. Whether you're an out-of-state investor or managing properties in your own backyard, having trusted professionals on the ground can mean the difference between a thriving portfolio and costly missteps. This chapter explores how to select, evaluate, and maintain strong relationships with local realtors and property managers to maximize your real estate investments.

7.1 The Importance of a Strong Local Team

A real estate investment is only as good as the people managing it. Even the best properties can under-perform if the wrong team is in place. A strong local team provides:

- **Market insights** – Local professionals understand trends, pricing, and rental demand.
- **Time savings** – A team allows you to focus on scaling your business rather than managing every detail.
- **Risk mitigation** – Experts help you avoid costly mistakes and legal pitfalls.
- **Operational efficiency** – Property managers handle daily operations, tenant relations, and maintenance.

7.2 Finding the Right Realtor

A skilled real estate agent specializing in investment properties can be invaluable in identifying lucrative opportunities, negotiating deals, and guiding you through the buying process. Here's how to find the right one:

7.2.1 Qualities of a Great Investment-Focused Realtor

- **Local Market Expertise** – The agent should have deep knowledge of the specific neighborhoods you're targeting.
- **Investor-Friendly Mindset** – Look for realtors who regularly work with investors and understand cash flow, cap rates, and ROI.
- **Negotiation Skills** – A great realtor can secure the best price and terms.
- **Access to Off-Market Deals** – Well-connected agents can bring you deals before they hit the MLS.

7.2.2 How to Vet and Select a Realtor

- **Ask for Referrals** – Network with other investors for recommendations.
- **Review Past Transactions** – Check if they have experience in investment properties.
- **Interview Multiple Agents** – Ask about their strategy for finding deals and how they assist investors.
- **Request a Sample Deal Analysis** – See how they assess a property's potential profitability.

7.3 The Role of a Property Manager

Once you acquire properties, an effective property manager ensures they remain profitable. They handle tenant placement, rent collection, maintenance, and legal compliance.

7.3.1 Responsibilities of a Property Manager

- **Marketing and Leasing** – Advertising vacancies, screening tenants, and executing leases.
- **Rent Collection and Financial Management** – Ensuring on-time payments and managing expenses.
- **Property Maintenance and Repairs** – Coordinating repairs and inspections to maintain asset value.
- **Legal Compliance** – Keeping up with landlord-tenant laws and evictions when necessary.

7.3.2 How to Find and Evaluate a Property Manager

- **Look for Licensed and Accredited Managers** – Check if they belong to organizations like the National Association of Residential Property Managers (NARPM).

- **Understand Their Fee Structure** – Compare management fees, leasing fees, and maintenance costs.
- **Check Their Tenant Screening Process** – A strong screening process ensures quality tenants.
- **Request a Sample Monthly Report** – A good manager provides clear financial reports.
- **Read Online Reviews and Ask for References** – Check their reputation with other investors.

7.4 Building a Strong Relationship with Your Team

Finding great professionals is just the first step. Keeping them motivated and aligned with your investment goals ensures long-term success.

7.4.1 Communicate Your Goals Clearly

- Share your investment strategy and long-term vision.
- Ensure your realtor knows whether you prioritize cash flow, appreciation, or a mix.
- Let your property manager know your preferred maintenance standards and tenant expectations.

7.4.2 Establish Trust and Accountability

- **Set Expectations Upfront** – Clearly define responsibilities, response times, and reporting methods.
- **Use Contracts and Agreements** – Formalize terms to avoid misunderstandings.
- **Schedule Regular Check-Ins** – Monthly or quarterly meetings help keep everyone aligned.

7.4.3 Reward Performance and Maintain Loyalty

- Provide bonuses or incentives for outstanding performance.
- Give referrals to realtors and property managers who exceed expectations.
- Treat your team with respect and professionalism.

7.5 What to Do If You Need to Replace Team Members

Sometimes, a team member may not meet expectations. Here's how to handle it professionally:

- **Address Issues Early** – Provide feedback and allow them to improve.
- **Review Your Contracts** – Ensure you follow termination clauses if needed.
- **Have a Backup Plan** – Maintain relationships with multiple professionals in case you need a replacement.

7.6 Conclusion

Your real estate business is only as strong as the local team supporting it. By carefully selecting and maintaining relationships with skilled realtors and property managers, you position yourself for long-term success, higher profitability, and smoother operations. Investing time into building this network now will pay dividends for years to come.

| 8 |

Handling Maintenance and Repairs From Afar

Coordinating Services Remotely
Without Compromising Quality

Introduction

Managing maintenance and repairs from a distance is one of the biggest challenges for real estate investors, especially those with properties spread across multiple locations. However, with the right systems in place, you can ensure high-quality service without being physically present. This chapter will cover strategies for remotely handling maintenance and repairs efficiently, including setting up a reliable network of service providers, leveraging technology, and implementing proactive maintenance plans.

1. Establish a Reliable Network of Local Contractors

Having a trusted team of local professionals is essential for managing maintenance remotely. This network should include:

- **General contractors** for larger projects and renovations.
- **Handymen** for minor repairs and quick fixes.
- **Specialists** (plumbers, electricians, HVAC technicians) for complex repairs.
- **Landscapers and cleaners** for curb appeal and tenant turnovers.

Tips for Finding and Vetting Contractors:

- **Get referrals** from other local property owners, real estate agents, or property managers.
- **Use online directories and platforms** such as Angie's List, Thumbtack, and HomeAdvisor.
- **Check reviews and references** from previous clients.
- **Request proof of licensing and insurance** to protect against liability.
- **Set up trial projects** before committing to long-term relationships.

2. Implement a Digital Work Order System

A structured system for handling maintenance requests ensures timely responses and efficient service. Consider using:

- **Property management software** (e.g., Buildium, AppFolio, RentRedi) to receive, assign, and track repairs.
- **Maintenance request portals** where tenants can submit issues with photos and descriptions.

- **Automated workflows** to assign tasks to preferred vendors based on issue type.

3. Build an Emergency Response Plan

Emergencies such as water leaks, heating failures, or electrical issues require immediate action. Have a plan in place to address urgent problems without delays.

Key Steps:

- Provide tenants with a list of approved emergency contacts.
- Establish a 24/7 hotline or service provider for after-hours issues.
- Authorize a property manager or local representative to handle urgent repairs up to a set dollar amount.

4. Conduct Routine and Preventative Maintenance

Preventative maintenance reduces the likelihood of costly emergency repairs. Set up regular inspections and servicing for:

- **HVAC systems** (filters, seasonal servicing).
- **Plumbing** (check for leaks, inspect water heaters).
- **Roof and gutters** (especially after storms).
- **Electrical systems** (circuit breakers, outlets).
- **Appliances** (cleaning and routine servicing).

Schedule vendors for regular visits and use **maintenance tracking software** to log completed work.

5. Leverage Smart Home Technology for Remote Monitoring

Smart technology allows property owners to keep an eye on their properties from anywhere. Consider:

- **Smart thermostats** to control heating and cooling remotely.
- **Leak detectors** that alert you to potential water damage.
- **Security cameras** to monitor property exteriors and shared spaces.
- **Smart locks** to grant vendors or tenants access without physical keys.

These tools provide real-time updates and reduce the need for in-person inspections.

6. Communicate Clearly with Tenants

Good tenant relationships lead to better property care and fewer maintenance surprises.

- **Set clear expectations** in the lease regarding maintenance requests and response times.
- **Encourage tenants to report minor issues early** to prevent major damage.
- **Provide an easy-to-use communication channel** (e.g., a tenant portal, email, or dedicated phone line).

7. Hire a Property Manager (If Needed)

If you own multiple units or don't have time to oversee maintenance, a **property manager** can handle repairs, vendor coordination, and tenant communication on your behalf.

- Choose a manager with a strong local reputation.
- Ensure they provide **detailed maintenance reports** regularly.
- Negotiate a fair management fee that aligns with your profit goals.

8. Create a Maintenance Reserve Fund

Unexpected repairs can be financially draining. To avoid cash flow issues, set aside a **maintenance reserve fund** equal to:

- **1%–3% of the property's value per year** for maintenance expenses.
- **A contingency fund for major replacements**, such as HVAC or roofing.

Conclusion: A Systematic Approach to Remote Maintenance

Handling maintenance remotely doesn't have to be stressful. By establishing **a network of trusted professionals, leveraging technology, implementing preventative maintenance, and maintaining clear tenant communication**, you can ensure that repairs are managed efficiently without compromising quality. A well-maintained property not only retains its value but also keeps tenants happy, reducing turnover and increasing long-term profitability.

| 9 |

Marketing Your Rentals Remotely

Effective Digital Marketing Strategies to Attract Tenants

Introduction

As a remote rental property owner, mastering digital marketing is essential to attract high-quality tenants quickly and efficiently. In this chapter, we'll cover key strategies, tools, and best practices for marketing your rental properties remotely, ensuring maximum visibility and minimal vacancy time.

9.1 The Power of Digital Marketing for Remote Landlords

Marketing your rentals remotely is not just about listing your property—it's about creating a strong online presence, leveraging technology, and strategically targeting the right audience. Digital marketing allows landlords to:

- Reach a broader tenant pool
- Showcase properties professionally through media-rich content
- Automate lead generation and screening
- Reduce vacancies through consistent marketing efforts

9.2 Creating a Standout Online Rental Listing

Your rental listing is your first impression. A well-crafted listing should include:

- **A Compelling Headline**
  Example: *"Modern 2-Bedroom Apartment with Skyline Views – Available Now!"*
- **High-Quality Photos & Videos**
  - Use natural lighting for photos
  - Capture wide-angle shots of all rooms
  - Include exterior and neighborhood images
  - Offer a video walkthrough or 3D tour
- **Detailed Property Description**
  - Highlight key features (e.g., smart home technology, pet-friendly, utilities included)
  - Mention nearby amenities, public transportation, and schools
  - Clearly outline rental terms (e.g., lease duration, deposit, pet policy)

- **Transparent Pricing & Fees**
  - Specify rent amount, security deposit, and any additional costs
  - Include move-in specials or discounts (if applicable)

9.3 Leveraging Listing Platforms to Maximize Exposure

To increase visibility, list your property on multiple rental platforms:

- **General Listing Sites**
  - Zillow Rentals, Apartments.com, Rent.com, Craigslist, Facebook Marketplace
- **Niche Platforms (For Specific Audiences)**
  - Furnished Finder (for traveling professionals)
  - Airbnb & Vrbo (for short-term rentals)
  - HousingAnywhere (for international renters)
  - PadSplit (for co-living spaces)
- **MLS & Realtor Networks**
  - Work with local real estate agents to get listings on the MLS

Pro Tip: Automate syndication using software like Avail, RentRedi, or Buildium to distribute your listing across multiple platforms at once.

9.4 Social Media Marketing: Attracting Tenants Through Engagement

Social media is a powerful tool for remote landlords. Utilize:

- **Facebook & Instagram**
  - Post high-quality photos, stories, and reels of the property

- Run Facebook Marketplace rental ads targeting specific demographics
- Join local housing groups and engage with potential tenants
- **TikTok & YouTube**
  - Share property tours, tenant testimonials, and neighborhood highlights
  - Create short-form videos showcasing the best features of your rental
- **LinkedIn (for Corporate & Executive Rentals)**
  - Network with relocation specialists and HR managers seeking housing for employees
- **Pinterest**
  - Create property boards showcasing interior design, nearby attractions, and rental tips

Pro Tip: Use hashtags like #ForRent, #ApartmentLiving, #RentalHomes, and location-specific tags to increase reach.

9.5 Paid Advertising: Reaching the Right Tenants Faster

If you want to fill vacancies quickly, paid advertising can help:

- **Google Ads**
  - Target searches like *"2-bedroom apartment in Springfield IL"*
  - Use location-based targeting to reach renters searching in your area
- **Facebook & Instagram Ads**
  - Run geo-targeted campaigns for specific demographics (e.g., young professionals, students)
- **Zillow & Apartments.com Boosted Listings**

    ○ Paid placements increase exposure and show your rental above standard listings

Pro Tip: Retarget visitors who viewed your listing but didn't inquire using Facebook Pixel or Google remarketing ads.

9.6 Virtual Tours & 3D Showings: The Remote Landlord's Secret Weapon

Offering virtual showings can significantly reduce the need for in-person tours. Use:

- **3D Virtual Tours** – Platforms like Matterport or Zillow 3D Home create interactive tours
- **Live Video Tours** – Offer FaceTime, Zoom, or WhatsApp tours for remote applicants
- **Pre-Recorded Video Walkthroughs** – Upload to YouTube and embed in listings

Pro Tip: Include a narrated walkthrough in your video to highlight key features.

9.7 Automating Lead Capture & Tenant Screening

To streamline your marketing efforts, automate the process:

- **Use Lead Capture Forms** – Google Forms or JotForm to collect inquiries
- **Automate Responses with Chatbots** – Set up chatbots on Facebook Messenger to answer FAQs
- **Implement Online Scheduling** – Use Calendly or Tenant-Turner for self-scheduled tours

- **Conduct Online Applications & Background Checks** – RentSpree, Zillow, or TurboTenant allow online applications and credit/background screenings

Pro Tip: Filter leads by requiring pre-qualifications before scheduling showings.

9.8 Building a Strong Online Reputation: Reviews & Testimonials

Positive tenant reviews can boost credibility and attract quality renters.

- Encourage satisfied tenants to leave reviews on Google, Facebook, or Yelp
- Showcase testimonials on your website and listings
- Respond to negative reviews professionally to maintain a good reputation

9.9 Email & SMS Marketing for Tenant Retention & Referrals

Keep a database of current and past tenants to:

- Offer renewal incentives
- Send seasonal maintenance reminders
- Promote referral programs (e.g., $100 rent credit for referring a new tenant)

Pro Tip: Use email automation software like Mailchimp or Active-Campaign to nurture leads.

9.10 Analyzing & Optimizing Your Marketing Strategy

Track performance to improve your marketing efforts:

- **Monitor Listing Views & Inquiries** – Check platform analytics to see where leads come from
- **A/B Test Different Listings & Ads** – Experiment with different headlines, descriptions, and images
- **Adjust Pricing & Promotions** – Use market data to stay competitive

Conclusion

Marketing your rentals remotely requires a combination of technology, automation, and strategic promotion. By leveraging listing platforms, social media, virtual tours, paid ads, and automation tools, you can attract quality tenants quickly and efficiently. The key is consistency—continuously optimizing your approach will keep vacancies low and rental income steady.

| 10 |

Legal Considerations for Remote Landlords

Staying Compliant With Landlord - Tenant Laws

Introduction

As a remote landlord, staying compliant with landlord-tenant laws is crucial to maintaining a successful rental business while avoiding costly legal disputes. Whether you manage properties across state lines or within the same jurisdiction, understanding and adhering to federal, state, and local regulations is key. This chapter outlines essential legal considerations, strategies for compliance, and best practices for managing your rental property legally from a distance.

1. Understanding Federal, State, and Local Landlord-Tenant Laws

Laws governing rental properties exist at multiple levels, and remote landlords must familiarize themselves with:

- **Federal Laws** – These include the **Fair Housing Act**, the **Americans with Disabilities Act (ADA)**, and other regulations that apply nationwide.
- **State Laws** – Each state has its own landlord-tenant laws that dictate security deposit limits, eviction procedures, habitability requirements, and lease agreement standards.
- **Local Ordinances** – Cities and counties may have additional rules regarding rent control, property inspections, and tenant protections.

Action Steps:

- Regularly review legal updates for each jurisdiction where you own property.
- Consult with a real estate attorney or property management firm to ensure compliance.
- Subscribe to local housing authority newsletters or legal updates.

2. Drafting Legally Sound Lease Agreements

A well-structured lease agreement is the foundation of legal compliance and protects both landlord and tenant interests.

Key Elements of a Strong Lease Agreement:

- **Clear Rental Terms** – Define rent amount, due dates, late fees, and acceptable payment methods.

- **Security Deposit Rules** – Specify deposit amounts, conditions for deductions, and refund timelines.
- **Maintenance and Repairs** – Detail tenant and landlord responsibilities for property upkeep.
- **Entry and Notice Requirements** – Outline how and when landlords can enter the property.
- **Termination and Eviction Terms** – Explain lease termination conditions, including notice periods and legal grounds for eviction.

Best Practices:

- Use state-specific lease agreements instead of generic templates.
- Ensure electronic lease agreements comply with **Electronic Signatures in Global and National Commerce (E-SIGN) Act** and **Uniform Electronic Transactions Act (UETA)** standards.
- Periodically update lease agreements to reflect changes in the law.

3. Fair Housing Compliance

The **Fair Housing Act (FHA)** prohibits discrimination based on race, color, national origin, religion, sex, disability, and familial status. Some states and cities extend protections to cover sexual orientation, gender identity, or source of income (e.g., Section 8 vouchers).

Compliance Strategies:

- Standardize tenant screening criteria to ensure consistency.
- Avoid discriminatory language in advertisements (e.g., "No kids" or "Ideal for professionals").
- Provide reasonable accommodations for tenants with disabilities (e.g., allowing service animals despite a no-pet policy).

Potential Legal Pitfalls:

- Discriminating based on income sources, which is illegal in some jurisdictions.
- Using criminal background checks in a way that violates HUD guidance on disparate impact.

4. Tenant Screening and Fair Application Processes

A structured screening process reduces the risk of discrimination claims and ensures you choose qualified tenants.

Legal Screening Criteria:

- Credit history
- Income verification (e.g., 3x rent rule)
- Rental history and landlord references
- Background checks (must comply with Fair Credit Reporting Act - FCRA)

Illegal Screening Practices:

- Rejecting tenants based on race, religion, or family status
- Using inconsistent criteria for different applicants
- Denying applicants solely based on past criminal records without assessing individual circumstances

Action Steps:

- Use third-party screening services that follow federal and state laws.
- Provide written explanations if rejecting an applicant based on background check results.

- Maintain records of all rental applications and reasons for approval or denial.

5. Security Deposits and Rent Collection Compliance

Each state has specific rules on handling security deposits, including:

- Maximum deposit amounts (often 1-2 months' rent)
- Timelines for returning deposits (typically 14-30 days)
- Requirements for holding deposits in separate escrow accounts

Legal Rent Collection Practices:

- Late fee limits and grace periods vary by state.
- Some jurisdictions require landlords to offer multiple payment options.
- Digital payment platforms (e.g., Zelle, Venmo, PayPal) may have restrictions on business transactions.

Best Practices:

- Provide a detailed move-in/move-out checklist to avoid disputes over deposit deductions.
- Follow proper notification procedures before deducting damages from a security deposit.
- Use rent collection platforms that offer automated payment tracking.

6. Property Maintenance and Habitability Standards

Landlords are legally required to maintain a habitable living environment.

Common Habitability Requirements:

- Adequate heating, plumbing, and electrical systems
- Compliance with building codes
- Pest control and mold prevention
- Functioning smoke and carbon monoxide detectors

Remote Management Strategies:

- Hire a local property manager or maintenance company to handle urgent repairs.
- Conduct virtual inspections or require tenants to submit periodic maintenance reports.
- Use home warranty services to streamline repair requests.

7. Understanding and Handling Evictions Legally

Evictions must follow strict legal procedures to avoid costly lawsuits.

Typical Eviction Process:

1. Provide a written **notice to cure** or **pay or quit** based on lease violations.
2. File an eviction lawsuit (unlawful detainer action) if the tenant fails to comply.
3. Attend court proceedings and obtain a judgment.
4. Use a sheriff or legal authority to enforce eviction—**self-help evictions (e.g., changing locks) are illegal.**

Alternative Solutions to Eviction:

- **Cash for keys** – Offer financial incentives for voluntary move-out.

- **Mediation services** – Work with local tenant-landlord resolution programs.
- **Payment plans** – Negotiate overdue rent before resorting to eviction.

Legal Risks to Avoid:

- Retaliatory evictions (e.g., evicting a tenant for reporting maintenance issues).
- Violating local COVID-19 rental protections (some cities still have eviction restrictions).
- Discriminatory eviction practices (e.g., targeting specific tenant demographics).

8. Hiring a Property Manager or Legal Advisor

For remote landlords, hiring local professionals can help ensure legal compliance.

Who to Consider Hiring:

- **Property Manager** – Handles day-to-day operations, tenant communication, and maintenance.
- **Real Estate Attorney** – Provides legal guidance on lease agreements, evictions, and fair housing laws.
- **Certified Public Accountant (CPA)** – Ensures compliance with rental property tax laws.

Best Practices:

- Use a licensed property manager familiar with local regulations.
- Set clear terms in property management contracts, including fees and responsibilities.
- Periodically review legal and tax compliance with professionals.

Conclusion

Navigating legal responsibilities as a remote landlord requires diligence, proactive planning, and access to reliable local resources. By staying informed about landlord-tenant laws, implementing legally sound lease agreements, and maintaining compliance with fair housing and eviction regulations, you can operate your rental business smoothly while avoiding legal pitfalls.

Key Takeaways:

- Keep up with federal, state, and local housing laws.
- Use standardized, legally compliant lease agreements.
- Follow fair housing and tenant screening best practices.
- Maintain proper security deposit and rent collection procedures.
- Handle maintenance and habitability issues promptly.
- Follow due process for evictions to avoid legal consequences.
- Consider hiring professionals to assist with property management and legal compliance.

By implementing these best practices, you can ensure long-term success as a legally compliant and profitable remote landlord.

| 11 |

Scaling Your Rental Portfolio Remotely

Expanding Investments Without Geographical Limitations

Introduction

Expanding your rental portfolio beyond your local market is a powerful way to increase cash flow, diversify risk, and capitalize on high-growth real estate markets. With technology, strong systems, and the right team in place, investors can successfully manage rental properties from anywhere in the world. This chapter will explore strategies, tools, and best practices for remote real estate investing while minimizing risk and maximizing profitability.

1. Why Expand Beyond Your Local Market?

Not every local market offers the best conditions for real estate investing. Some reasons to look elsewhere include:

- **Higher Cash Flow Potential** – Some markets offer better rent-to-price ratios.
- **Diversification** – Investing in multiple markets reduces risk tied to a single economy.
- **Lower Property Costs** – Expanding can help you find affordable properties with better ROI.
- **Better Landlord-Friendly Laws** – Some states and cities have laws that are more favorable to landlords.
- **More Growth Potential** – Certain markets experience rapid appreciation and development.

2. Choosing the Right Market

Finding the best markets for remote real estate investing requires research and analysis. Here's how to identify the right location:

A. Key Market Indicators

- **Population Growth** – A growing population often leads to increasing rental demand.
- **Job Market & Economy** – Strong employment opportunities attract renters.
- **Median Home Price & Rent** – Look for markets with a good rent-to-price ratio.
- **Vacancy Rates** – Low vacancies indicate strong demand.
- **Property Taxes & Insurance Costs** – Lower expenses improve profit margins.

B. Best Sources for Market Research

- **Zillow & Redfin** – Home prices, rental rates, and market trends.
- **City Data & Census.gov** – Population growth and demographics.
- **BiggerPockets Market Insights** – Investor discussions and market analysis.
- **Realtor.com & Rentometer** – Rental rate comparisons.

C. Hot Real Estate Markets for Remote Investing

- **Midwest & Southeast** – Cities like Indianapolis, Memphis, and Birmingham offer low-cost, high-cash-flow properties.
- **Texas & Florida** – Business-friendly states with strong economic growth.
- **Secondary & Tertiary Markets** – Smaller cities with growing demand.

3. Building a Local Team

Since you won't be physically present, having a strong local team is essential. Your key players include:

A. Property Management Company

- Collects rent, handles maintenance, and manages tenants.
- Look for companies with positive reviews and transparent fees.

B. Real Estate Agents & Wholesalers

- Help identify off-market deals and negotiate better prices.
- Seek agents specializing in investor-friendly properties.

C. Contractors & Maintenance Teams

- A reliable network for repairs and renovations.
- Consider third-party inspection services to verify work quality.

D. Attorneys & Title Companies

- Handle legal aspects of property transactions and leases.
- Ensure compliance with local laws.

E. Lenders & Financing Options

- Explore DSCR loans, commercial loans, and private lenders for financing.

4. Acquiring Properties Remotely

A. Finding Deals

- **MLS & Realtor Networks** – Use local agents to access MLS listings.
- **Wholesale & Off-Market Deals** – Join real estate investment groups.
- **Online Marketplaces** – Roofstock, LoopNet, and Auction.com specialize in investor properties.

B. Due Diligence

- **Virtual Tours & Inspections** – Use video walkthroughs, Matterport, or local inspectors.
- **Hire Local Inspectors** – Conduct a thorough home inspection before purchase.
- **Financial Analysis** – Ensure the property meets your cash flow and ROI requirements.

C. Financing Your Remote Investments

- **Conventional & DSCR Loans** – Loans based on rental income.
- **Portfolio Loans** – For purchasing multiple properties.
- **Seller Financing & Private Lending** – Creative financing options to minimize upfront capital.

5. Remote Property Management & Operations

Once you own properties remotely, managing them effectively is crucial.

A. Leveraging Technology

- **Property Management Software** – Tools like Buildium, AppFolio, and RentRedi streamline tenant communication, rent collection, and maintenance.
- **Smart Home Technology** – Use smart locks, security cameras, and thermostats for remote monitoring.

B. Handling Repairs & Maintenance

- **Service Agreements** – Pre-arrange contracts with local repair professionals.
- **Emergency Protocols** – Have a plan for urgent maintenance issues.

C. Managing Tenants from Afar

- **Screen Tenants Thoroughly** – Use online screening tools like TransUnion SmartMove.
- **Clear Lease Agreements** – Ensure leases are detailed and enforceable.

- **Maintain Strong Communication** – Regularly check in with your property manager and tenants.

6. Scaling Your Portfolio Efficiently

A. Automating Processes

- **Use Virtual Assistants** – They can help with admin work, lease renewals, and data management.
- **Automate Rent Collection** – Use online payment portals to streamline payments.

B. Refinancing & Reinvesting

- **Cash-Out Refinancing** – Pull equity from existing properties to fund new acquisitions.
- **BRRRR Strategy** – Buy, Rehab, Rent, Refinance, Repeat to scale faster.

C. Portfolio Diversification

- Invest in different states or property types (e.g., single-family, multifamily, or short-term rentals) to spread risk.

7. Avoiding Common Pitfalls

A. Overpaying for Properties

- Always compare rental comps and home values before buying.

B. Poor Property Management

- Vet property managers carefully and set clear expectations.

C. Underestimating Expenses

- Budget for property taxes, insurance, repairs, and vacancies.

D. Lack of Market Knowledge

- Stay updated on local laws, economic trends, and rental regulations.

Final Thoughts

Scaling a rental portfolio remotely is more feasible than ever with the right strategies, tools, and team in place. By leveraging technology, selecting the right markets, and building a reliable local team, you can expand your investments beyond geographical limitations while maintaining control and profitability.

Key Takeaways:

- Research markets carefully to find strong cash-flowing areas.

- Build a reliable team, including property managers, agents, and contractors.

- Use technology to streamline management and tenant communication.

- Automate processes to save time and scale faster.

- Avoid common pitfalls by conducting thorough due diligence.

By implementing these strategies, you can build a robust rental portfolio that generates passive income no matter where you are.

| 12 |

Crisis Management for Remote Landlord

Handling Emergencies and Tenant Disputes from a Distance

Introduction

Managing rental properties remotely presents unique challenges, especially when crises arise. Whether it's a sudden maintenance emergency, a legal dispute, or a tenant conflict, being prepared is essential for protecting your investment and ensuring tenant satisfaction. This chapter will guide you through best practices for handling emergencies and disputes from a distance while maintaining control and minimizing stress.

Section 1: Establishing an Emergency Response System

When you're a remote landlord, having a structured emergency response plan in place is critical. Emergencies can range from plumbing leaks to fire hazards and tenant-related incidents. Here's how to ensure you're ready:

1.1 Define What Constitutes an Emergency

Emergencies in rental properties typically fall into three categories:

- **Property Damage:** Flooding, fire, broken pipes, or storm damage.
- **Health & Safety Hazards:** Gas leaks, mold, electrical hazards, or pest infestations.
- **Tenant-Related Issues:** Criminal activity, domestic disputes, or medical emergencies.

1.2 Build a Reliable Vendor Network

Having a pre-vetted list of professionals available 24/7 ensures quick resolution of maintenance emergencies. Your vendor list should include:

- Plumbers
- Electricians
- HVAC specialists
- General contractors
- Locksmiths
- Pest control services

1.3 Partner with a Local Property Manager or Emergency Contact

If managing vendors remotely is difficult, consider hiring a local property manager or appointing a trusted individual to act on your behalf during emergencies. They should have access to:

- Spare keys
- Tenant contact information
- Your preferred vendor list

1.4 Implement a Clear Emergency Reporting System

Tenants should have an easy way to report emergencies, such as:

- A dedicated emergency phone line or voicemail
- An online maintenance portal
- An email designated for urgent issues

Clearly define what happens when they report an emergency, including response time expectations.

Section 2: Handling Maintenance Emergencies Remotely

2.1 Prioritizing and Assessing Urgency

Not all maintenance issues require immediate action. Use the following framework to classify and prioritize:

- **Immediate action required:** Burst pipes, electrical failures, or gas leaks.
- **Quick response (within 24 hours):** Broken heating during winter, major appliance failure.
- **Routine maintenance (within a week):** Leaky faucets, minor cosmetic damage.

2.2 Remote Troubleshooting

Sometimes, tenants can temporarily resolve issues until a professional arrives. Offer troubleshooting steps for:

- **Power outages:** Checking breaker boxes and resetting GFCI outlets.
- **Leaks:** Shutting off water supply valves.
- **HVAC issues:** Changing filters or checking the thermostat settings.

2.3 Utilizing Smart Technology

Smart home devices help landlords manage emergencies remotely:

- **Smart thermostats** prevent heating/cooling failures.
- **Smart water sensors** detect leaks early.
- **Security cameras** allow monitoring of vacant properties.

If you have access to these systems, you can diagnose problems before sending out a contractor.

Section 3: Managing Tenant Disputes from Afar

Tenant disputes can range from late rent payments to neighbor conflicts. Being proactive can help prevent minor issues from escalating.

3.1 Establishing Clear Communication Channels

Open, consistent communication prevents misunderstandings. Options include:

- Email or text messaging
- A tenant portal for logging complaints
- Scheduled check-ins via phone or video call

3.2 Enforcing Lease Agreements and Policies

Ensure that lease terms are clear on:

- **Rent payment deadlines and consequences for late payments**
- **Noise policies and neighbor relations**
- **Rules for property modifications or unauthorized occupants**

Refer to lease agreements when resolving disputes and avoid emotional reactions.

3.3 Dealing with Late Rent Payments

If a tenant falls behind on rent, take a structured approach:

1. **Send a polite reminder** after 1–3 days.
2. **Issue a formal late notice** (including any applicable late fees).
3. **Offer a payment plan** if they've been reliable in the past.
4. **Start the eviction process** only if necessary, following local laws.

Automated rent collection systems help prevent payment delays.

3.4 Mediating Tenant Conflicts

Neighbor disputes or conflicts with roommates can escalate quickly. As a remote landlord:

- Encourage tenants to resolve minor issues themselves.
- Provide written documentation of house rules.
- If necessary, intervene by speaking with both parties and offering mediation.

For legal issues or harassment cases, involve law enforcement or legal counsel.

Section 4: Handling Legal and Eviction Situations Remotely

4.1 Understanding Local Landlord-Tenant Laws

Since landlord-tenant laws vary by state and city, staying informed is crucial. Resources include:

- Local housing authority websites
- Online legal databases
- A real estate attorney for guidance

4.2 Using Property Management or Legal Services for Evictions

Evictions can be time-consuming, especially from a distance. If eviction is unavoidable:

- Hire a local attorney or property manager to handle court proceedings.
- Send all notices via certified mail for documentation.
- Follow proper legal protocols to avoid delays or tenant claims.

If eviction isn't feasible, consider a **cash-for-keys agreement**—offering money for voluntary move-out to avoid court proceedings.

Section 5: Preventative Measures to Minimize Future Crises

5.1 Conducting Thorough Tenant Screening

Many crises stem from problematic tenants. Reduce risks by:

- Running credit and background checks
- Checking rental history and references
- Ensuring financial stability through proof of income

5.2 Scheduling Regular Property Inspections

Preventative maintenance prevents costly emergencies. If you can't visit in person:

- Arrange for a local inspector to check on the property quarterly.
- Require tenants to report maintenance issues before they escalate.

5.3 Investing in a Home Warranty Plan

A home warranty covers major repairs and can reduce out-of-pocket expenses for:

- HVAC systems
- Electrical issues
- Plumbing failures
- Appliance repairs

Conclusion: Building a Crisis-Resilient Remote Rental Business

Remote property management is all about **preparedness, communication, and delegation**. By setting up an emergency response system, handling disputes professionally, and utilizing technology, you can confidently manage your rentals from anywhere. Being proactive, rather than reactive, ensures that both your property and tenant relationships remain stable—no matter where you are.

| 13 |

Working With Local Housing Authorities

Introduction

Partnering with local housing authorities through the Section 8 Housing Choice Voucher (HCV) program can provide landlords with a stable and reliable rental income stream. As a federally funded program operating nationwide, Section 8 enables qualified tenants to receive rental assistance while offering landlords guaranteed payments directly from the housing authority. This program is particularly beneficial for remote landlords, as it includes built-in safeguards such as tenant screening, rental payment security, and housing quality inspections.

Understanding the Housing Choice Voucher Program

The Section 8 program is designed to help low-income families, the elderly, and individuals with disabilities afford safe and decent housing in the private market. Through this initiative, tenants receive a housing voucher that covers a portion of their rent, with the balance paid directly to the landlord. One of the major advantages of this program is that tenants can transfer their assistance from one jurisdiction to another, allowing landlords access to a larger pool of potential renters.

Benefits for Landlords

For landlords, working with local housing authorities offers several advantages, including:

1. Guaranteed Rental Payments

One of the most attractive aspects of the Section 8 program is the guaranteed rental payments made directly by the housing authority. This reduces the risk of missed or late rent payments, providing a more predictable cash flow.

2. Tenant Prescreening and Stability

Housing authorities conduct background checks and verify income before issuing vouchers to tenants. This pre-screening process can help landlords secure reliable tenants. Additionally, since tenants risk losing their assistance if they violate program rules or fail to pay their share of the rent, they are often incentivized to be responsible renters.

3. Regular Property Inspections and Quality Control

Housing authorities conduct annual or biennial inspections to ensure rental units meet HUD's Housing Quality Standards (HQS). While some landlords may view inspections as a hassle, they help maintain property value and ensure that tenants live in safe conditions. This quality control process can lead to fewer maintenance issues and better property upkeep over time.

4. Rent Increases and Market Adjustments

Most housing authorities allow landlords to request rent increases based on fair market rents. These adjustments ensure that landlords receive competitive rental income over time while keeping their properties within an affordable range for voucher holders.

5. Paperless Leasing and Streamlined Processes

Many housing authorities are transitioning to digital platforms for applications, leasing, and communication. This makes it easier for landlords—especially those operating remotely—to submit documents, complete property inspections, and manage tenant-related paperwork without the need for in-person visits.

6. Access to a Large Pool of Tenants

With increasing demand for affordable housing, landlords participating in the Section 8 program often experience high occupancy rates and low vacancy periods. This means less downtime between tenants and a steady rental income.

Challenges to Consider

While the benefits are substantial, landlords should also be aware of potential challenges when working with local housing authorities:

- **Inspection Requirements**: Units must pass an initial inspection and periodic re-inspections. If a unit fails, landlords must make the necessary repairs before leasing.
- **Rent Limitations**: Housing authorities set rent limits based on Fair Market Rents (FMR), which may sometimes be lower than what a landlord could charge a private-paying tenant.
- **Tenant Issues**: Although tenants are screened by the housing authority, landlords must still conduct their own due diligence, as eviction processes can be complicated for voucher holders.

- **Administrative Delays**: Some housing authorities may have slow processing times for approvals, inspections, or payments. Understanding the process and working with an efficient housing authority can minimize delays.

How to Get Started as a Section 8 Landlord

1. **Contact Your Local Housing Authority**: Reach out to the housing authority in your area to learn about their specific requirements and registration process.
2. **Ensure Your Property Meets Requirements**: Your rental unit must meet HUD's Housing Quality Standards before tenants can move in. Address any necessary repairs before the inspection.
3. **Set Competitive Rent**: Check the Fair Market Rent (FMR) in your area to ensure your rent aligns with the housing authority guidelines.
4. **Advertise Your Property**: Many housing authorities have online portals where landlords can list their available units for voucher holders.
5. **Screen Tenants Thoroughly**: Even though the housing authority screens tenants, landlords should still conduct their own background and rental history checks.
6. **Sign a Lease Agreement**: The lease agreement must comply with HUD and local housing authority regulations. Once signed, the landlord will receive direct payments from the housing authority.

Conclusion

Working with local housing authorities through the Section 8 Housing Choice Voucher program can be a valuable strategy for landlords looking to secure long-term, stable rental income. By understanding

the benefits, challenges, and best practices, landlords—especially remote investors—can leverage this federally backed program to maintain occupancy, reduce financial risks, and contribute to providing
affordable housing in their communities.

| 14 |

Evictions & Administrative Hearings

Introduction

Unfortunately, evictions are a part of the reality of being a landlord. While no landlord enters this business hoping to remove tenants from a property, there are times when it becomes a necessary step to protect your investment. In addition to evictions, landlords may also find themselves summoned to administrative hearings involving city code violations, nuisance complaints, or local ordinance compliance. These hearings may require your physical presence or that of a legal representative, especially if you are managing your properties remotely.

Avoiding Eviction Through Prevention

The best eviction is the one that never happens. By establishing a strong tenant screening and application process, you can greatly reduce your exposure to high-risk tenants. Look for red flags during the screening process: prior evictions, inconsistent income, or incomplete application information. Require employment verification, rental history, credit checks, and references. Clearly explain your lease terms, expectations, and consequences for non-compliance during the move-in process.

Also, include a clause in your lease outlining the eviction process and grounds for removal. Tenants who understand the rules upfront are less likely to violate them later.

When Eviction Becomes Necessary

Even with the best screening process, issues can arise. Life circumstances, job loss, relationship breakdowns, or health problems can all contribute to late or non-payment. While compassion is important, as a remote landlord, you must also treat your rental business like a business.

The most common reason for eviction is **non-payment of rent**. However, **lease violations**—such as unauthorized occupants, illegal activity, excessive noise, or property damage—should be taken just as seriously. A pattern of lease breaches can compromise the safety and comfort of your other tenants and your property's long-term value.

Act swiftly when problems emerge. Don't allow unpaid rent to stack up or lease violations to go unchecked. Delay often results in greater losses, especially when you're operating from a distance.

Alternatives to Formal Eviction

Formal evictions are costly, time-consuming, and emotionally draining. One effective alternative is offering tenants **"Cash for Keys"**—a small financial incentive in exchange for vacating the property quickly and peacefully. While it may feel counter-intuitive to pay someone to leave, it can be much more efficient and less expensive than going through the legal eviction process.

This approach also helps you regain control of the property faster, saving time, legal fees, and potential property damage from a disgruntled tenant.

The Legal Eviction Process

If alternatives don't work and you must proceed with an eviction, it's critical to follow your state and local laws precisely. The process typically involves:

1. **Notice of Default & Opportunity to Cure**
   This is the first formal notice informing the tenant of the problem (non-payment, violation, etc.) and giving them a chance to fix it within a specified time frame. This could be a 3-Day, 5-Day, 7-Day, or even 10-Day Notice, depending on your jurisdiction.

2. **Filing for Eviction in Court**
   If the issue is not resolved, you must file an eviction lawsuit—commonly called an **Unlawful Detainer Action**. A court date will be set, and the tenant will be officially served with the lawsuit.

3. **Court Hearing & Judgment**
   At the hearing, the judge will decide whether to grant possession back to the landlord. The tenant may be given a final deadline to vacate the premises.

4. **Sheriff's Lockout (If Necessary)**
   If the tenant still refuses to leave after a court order, only a sheriff can physically remove them from the property. You, as the landlord, **cannot** remove the tenant yourself under any circumstances.

Your Role as a Remote Landlord

As a remote landlord, your ability—or obligation—to appear in court may depend on how the property is titled. For example, if the property is held under an LLC, the court may require legal representation. If the title is under your personal name, you might be required to appear yourself or assign Power of Attorney to a representative.

It's wise to build relationships with a local property manager, attorney, or eviction service who can represent your interests on the ground when you're not physically present.

Administrative Hearings & Code Compliance

Aside from tenant issues, landlords may occasionally be summoned to **administrative hearings** related to city code violations, zoning issues, nuisance complaints, or local ordinances. These could stem from issues like:

- Overgrown grass or trash accumulation
- Un-permitted work or construction
- Fire or safety violations
- Excessive noise complaints or criminal activity

These hearings may be scheduled with the city's building department, zoning board, or housing authority, and should be taken seriously. Failing to appear or respond could lead to fines, liens, or even condemnation proceedings.

Whenever possible, keep your properties in compliance with local codes. Schedule regular inspections, respond to neighbor complaints promptly, and maintain open lines of communication with city officials.

Key Takeaways:

- Use strong tenant screening to minimize eviction risks.
- Move quickly and strategically when issues arise—delay costs money.
- Consider "Cash for Keys" as a peaceful resolution to avoid court.
- Follow proper legal procedures for eviction; never self-evict.
- Know your obligations in administrative hearings—especially when managing remotely

| 15 |

Squatters: Prevention and Response

Introduction

As a Remote Landlord, one of your greatest fears may be discovering that someone has unlawfully taken possession of one of your vacant properties. Squatting—when an unauthorized person occupies a property without the owner's consent—can lead to costly legal battles, loss of rental income, and even property damage. Fortunately, there are smart preventive strategies and decisive actions you can take to protect your investments—even from a distance.

What is a Squatter?

A squatter is someone who enters and occupies a vacant property without a legal lease, rental agreement, or permission. While the term sometimes conjures images of desperate or displaced individuals, squatters can range from opportunistic trespassers to organized groups with knowledge of legal loopholes.

Preventive Measures for Remote Landlords

Preventing squatters is often easier and cheaper than removing them. Consider incorporating the following tools and strategies into your remote property management system:

1. Install Surveillance Cameras

- **Smart Security Systems:** Use motion-detecting, cloud-connected security cameras to monitor the exterior and interior (if unoccupied) of your property.
- **Remote Monitoring:** Choose systems that allow you to receive real-time alerts and live footage from your smartphone or laptop.
- **Visible Deterrents:** Place signage clearly stating that video surveillance is active—this alone can scare off potential squatters.

2. Utility "Revert to Owner" Agreements

- Work with utility companies to ensure that services such as electricity and water revert to your name automatically when a tenant moves out.
- Maintaining active utilities can make it easier to monitor the property (e.g., keep heat on to prevent pipe damage), while also helping avoid the tell-tale signs of vacancy that attract squatters.

3. Keyless Entry and Remote Access Locks

- **Smart Locks:** Install digital locks that can be controlled and monitored remotely. Change access codes instantly if a tenant moves out or if there's a suspected break-in.

- **Audit Trails:** Many smart lock systems maintain a log of entries and exits, providing helpful records in the event of unauthorized access.

4. Physical Presence & Property Checks

- Hire a local property manager or caretaker to inspect the property weekly.
- Use "For Rent" signs sparingly. While they attract renters, they also alert squatters that the property is vacant.
- Maintain curb appeal—overgrown lawns and accumulating mail are clear indicators that a property is unoccupied.

If You Discover Squatters: What Should You Do?

Stay calm and act legally. The worst thing you can do is take matters into your own hands. Most states have laws protecting even unauthorized occupants from illegal eviction tactics.

Step 1: Verify the Situation

- **Don't Assume:** Some squatters may present forged leases or claim tenancy. Document everything.
- **Consult Local Law:** Squatter rights vary by state. Some jurisdictions require a formal eviction even for trespassers if they've been in the property for a certain length of time.

Step 2: Call the Police

- If the squatter is clearly trespassing and has not established any legal rights to the property, law enforcement may be able to remove them immediately.

- Be prepared to show proof of ownership (title, deed, or tax bill) and documentation that the person is not a tenant (no lease, etc.).

Step 3: Serve Formal Notice

- If the police cannot remove the squatters, you'll likely need to go through a formal eviction process.
- This may include serving a **Notice to Vacate**, followed by a **court filing** for unlawful detainer.
- Hire a local attorney or eviction service to represent your interests if you're managing remotely.

Step 4: Document and Secure

- Take detailed photos and videos of the property's condition.
- Once the property is vacated, immediately change all locks, re-secure windows, and consider increasing surveillance and neighborhood awareness.

Final Thoughts

As a Remote Landlord, your success hinges on staying one step ahead of potential threats. Squatters can derail your cash flow and damage your reputation with neighbors and local governments. But with preventive systems in place and a well-rehearsed response strategy, you can minimize risk and keep your properties secure—even from hundreds of miles away.